Over The Fence!

Escaping Fear and Finding Success

Over The Fence!
Escaping Fear and Finding Success

By
Doug Ellingsworth

seven
ORDERS PRESS

Dyersburg, Tennessee

Copyright 2004© by Doug Ellingsworth

ISBN: 0-9706760-1-8

Seven Orders Press
Post Office Box 283
Dyersburg, TN 38025
www.sevenorders.com

This book is dedicated to those
Who refuse to fit in and go with the flow, and
Who are not afraid to stand out from the crowd
So that they can become everything
God created them to be.

Got BIG Dreams?

Congratulations! Far too many people give too little thought to their future. They bounce from one thing to another instead of establishing a plan that will lead them to contentment and satisfaction. But you know where you want to go, what you want to become. Wonderful! (Okay, maybe you don't know exactly, but keep reading anyway!)

But guess what? Living inside your head, parked next to where you keep all your dreams and ambitions, is the worst enemy of your success.

Sound crazy? Just wait until you start working on your plan. Thoughts will come running, telling you all the reasons why your dreams will never come true. Feelings you never experienced before will try to drown your hopes. Thoughts and feelings that are motivated by fear!

Fear has crippled more dreams than you can count. Fear is mean and has no favorites. It does not matter where you were born, how much money you have, or how big you are, fear lurks inside - waiting to foil your plans.

Fear completely overcomes some people. Ailurophobia (fear of cats), blennophobia (fear of slime), chionophobia (fear of snow), catoptrophobia (fear of mirrors), arachibutyrophobia (fear of peanut butter sticking to the roof of one's mouth), didaskaleinophobia (fear of school), homilophobia (fear of sermons), telephonophobia (fear of using the telephone) - are all real fears that render some people helpless.

While you may not be affected by these or any of the nearly four hundred phobias mental health professionals have cataloged, fear is a common emotion that you must conquer. Helping you defeat your personal fears is what this book is all about.

Nothing valuable is easily obtained. Dreams will never come true unless you work to help them along. So don't be discouraged when the road to your success gets a little rough and long. Keep on working and walking! Success belongs to those who refuse to let fear steal their dreams.

□

1   Just Say No!

Frank needed a vacation. The pace of the past year, while exhilarating, had demanded his best and most intense efforts for nearly 18 hours each day. He had received his party's nomination for Vice President of the United States. Being chosen to seek such an important office was a great honor and provided so many wonderful experiences, yet it had required Frank to be alert and mentally sharp every waking moment.

Now that the election was over and all the dust had settled, Frank headed north, as his family had for so many years, to enjoy some time in the great outdoors, swimming and fishing while his emotional and physical batteries recharged. The Republicans had come out on top during the general election, but Frank was only 39 years old and knew that many more opportunities and elections were in his future. His vacation would allow him more time to consider his options and decide just what to pursue next.

Having already served as the assistant to the Secretary of the Navy, Frank's talents were well known. He was the mastermind behind the anti-submarine plan that stopped the Germans control of the north Atlantic during World War I. When his time with the navy was finished, he returned home and was elected to the State Senate. From there his star rose until he was asked to represent his party as they sought to occupy our country's most important offices.

Losing this election was a new experience for Frank. He had always won. But being defeated did not tarnish his image. Doors of opportunity were swinging wider than ever before. Frank would have ample time to investigate them all while his family enjoyed their stay at their vacation home on a small Canadian island in the Bay of Fundy. That retreat was especially welcome in the summer of 1921.

Frank's vacation was interrupted by thick, black smoke drifting from forest fires burning on the other side of the island, so, along with two of his sons, he joined the battle against the blazes. Clearing firebreaks and wetting down underbrush was tiring work. The men labored for several hours in the heat and smoke until the fire was under control. The danger now past, Frank and his boys headed for home.

On the way back, Frank decided to cool off with a quick swim in the bay. After letting the cool sea water wash the soot and grime away, Frank joined his family in the house. As he walked inside, he noticed a bundle of mail waiting his attention. Still wearing his wet swimming clothes, Frank sat down and sorted through the pile and read the more urgent letters. A stack of newspapers had been delivered, so Frank thumbed through those.

A while later, feeling a cold coming on, Frank went to bed, thinking the extra rest would help to ward it off. But it was not going to be that easy. What Frank did not know as he closed his eyes that warm summer evening was that he had contracted the dreaded disease of polio!

For days Frank suffered severe pain and fever. His legs withered and became permanently paralyzed. As the months passed, exercise therapy, swimming, and various treatments helped him regain his strength. Eventually he would walk again, but his legs would have to be encased in steel braces and he would need a cane.

As the world looked on, it seemed that Frank was finished, his career doomed. But Frank was not giving up! Since he could no longer participate in normal physical activities, he worked on developing his mental skills. He refused to quit. He was not going to fade away. That determination was later reflected when he responded to someone's statement about a particularly difficult task that lay before him. "I once spent two years in bed trying to move my big toe," Frank said. "After that job, anything seems easy."

Seven years later, Frank became Governor of New York. In 1930, he was re-elected.

On March 4, 1933, Frank gave a speech that will be remembered as long as our nation survives. Our country was reeling during the first few months of the Great Depression, and his speech inspired confidence and courage in millions of folks who were fighting for their lives. The most memorable line struck right at the heart of the matter. "The only thing we have to fear is fear itself -- nameless, unreasoning, unjustified terror...."

Just a well-turned phrase by a crafty speech writer? Perhaps. But these words were spoken by a man who lived every day with the understanding that if the house caught on fire or if storms threatened, he could not run and hide. His lifeless legs would not carry him! Every terrible

5

possibility had passed through his mind. Frank had wrestled with fear for many years before he made that speech. Fear of rejection and ridicule, fear of losing his friends, fear of losing his position, fear of being left alone and unattended. These were a few of the fears that haunted him. But sometime, somewhere, during those years of struggle, Franklin Roosevelt determined that fear was not going to rule his life. His success proves that fear does not have the final word.

Just a well-turned phrase? Maybe. But who would better understand the threat and torment of fear than this man who whipped his own personal demons and became Governor of New York and the 32nd President of the United States?

And the speech? That was just his FIRST Inaugural Address! Franklin Roosevelt was elected President more times than any other person in our nation's history.

He understood that the greatest danger in being afraid is not that what you fear may actually occur, but rather that being frightened may keep you from chasing your dreams!

Don't be afraid to reach for the stars! Who knows what you can do until you try?

All you really have to fear is fear itself.

Frank ought to know!

□

2   I Love It! I Hate It!

Fear. Just a little word, but does it ever pack a wallop!

Fear keeps you from going outside alone after dark, but then seduces you into spending ten dollars to huddle with five friends inside a dark theater while it terrorizes the living daylights out of you! Go figure. Fear keeps you poor, but makes the movie-maker rich. And have you noticed that there are more scare-you-to-death books in the bookstore than there are books about, say, overcoming your worries?

When it comes to fear, we humans are funny characters. Sometimes we hate it; sometimes we love it. Some days we run from it; other days we run to it! We love to share the books and movies that frighten us with our best friends, but would never admit, even to our dearest friend, the personal fears that lurk deep inside our soul! Instead, we smile and act brave, as if nothing could ever frighten or intimidate us! But if we all revealed the secrets we work so hard to cover-up, not only would we see that we all battle fear, but that the fears we fight are probably the same ones!

There are plenty of things to be afraid of. Flying in airplanes, swimming in the ocean, spiders, going to the dentist, riding a roller coaster, changing schools, falling, and the list could go on forever. (Would you believe that getting fat ranks second on one list of common fears that Americans are most likely to admit?) But do you know what most teenagers fear most? It is not being alone in the dark or finding a snake in our bed, or any one of the fears in the list above. The thing we worry about the most is that we might make a fool of ourselves! It is not the threat of burglars that keeps us awake at night, but the thought of having to stand before an audience and give a speech steals our sleep!

Now you see why I say this fear business is a funny thing.

But funny or not, it is real. And it keeps far too many young people from pursuing their dreams.

There are a few secrets to overcoming fear. They are not really secrets - just principles, but they will work for you. These principles will help you overcome your fears and stay on the road to success.

Everyone has fears. You will find plenty of things to frighten you if you look for them. As a matter of fact, at this very moment researchers are busy trying to find more things for you to be afraid of! Some of those worries might keep you from pursuing your dreams. But even World Champion worriers can find success applying the principles discussed in these pages.

Don't let fear keep you trapped! Turn the page and begin your journey to success today!

□

3 Oops! I Messed Up!

So you are afraid that you might make a mistake. You might mess something up. You might make a wrong decision. You might (God forbid!) embarrass yourself!

So you are going to just sit there and do nothing?

Come on! How bad can it get? Say you do mess up. What is the worst that can happen? You've got to be real good at messing up to get to the top of the list!

In the fall of 1999, experts at NASA's Jet Propulsion Laboratory were proudly tracking the progress of the much-heralded Mars Polar Orbiter. This $125 million spacecraft was designed to orbit Mars and transmit ground-breaking scientific news back to its handlers on earth. The sleek rocket had been racing toward The Red Planet since its launch the previous December. After traveling more than 415 million miles in its nine-month journey, the spacecraft was poised to enter its first orbit around Mars when it accidentally flew too low toward Mars. The brave little rocket burned up in the thin Martian atmosphere.

The scientists were puzzled. What could have possibly gone wrong? They possessed the brightest minds, the latest technology, the biggest purse. It must have been a quirk of nature, some freak unpreventable accident.

A review of the final days of the little rocket's life revealed that the two major teams working on the project failed to communicate on one minor detail. The scientists who designed the craft sent instructions to the Mission Control navigators in English terms - like pounds per second of force. The navigation team assumed the measurements were metric - since they always use the metric system in their work. So their computers guided the rocket using grams per second of force . . . and the space history that would have been was not. And NASA (translation: American taxpayers) was out $125 million.

You think you can beat that? Whatever you are afraid might happen is going to be more expensive or embarrassing than that?

Enter the auditors from a major independent accounting firm hired to examine NASA's financial records that same year. They reviewed the records and shipped their report off to the House of Representatives Science Committee. As they were poring over the books, the committee discovered that NASA's accountants had failed to account for a few dollars. A few dollars . . . as in $590 million! And the big-time auditors had completely missed it! We aren't talking idiots here. These NASA folks are the ones who put a man on the moon, get the Space Shuttle up and down, link up with the orbiting Space Station every once in a while, and fix satellites while circling the earth. But they

10

somehow lost $590 million! And some of the world's finest accountants didn't even notice!

And you are afraid of embarrassing yourself? You think you might make a mistake? Come on! You've got to really be something to top these guys!

How do you think these accounting experts feel? Aren't they known for their nitpicking accuracy? Especially those good enough to be hired to audit government agencies! But do you think any of them quit because they made a mistake?

In August 2001, the Internal Revenue Service admitted that they had received over 21,000 complaints from taxpayers that the IRS had not cashed their checks. They weren't cashed because the IRS doesn't know where they are! They think some bank in Pennsylvania that they hired to handle tax receipts lost them. They hope to find them some day because those checks add up to about 810 million dollars!

Still afraid you might mess up?

In September 2001, the Social Security Administration admitted that they had paid $31 million to dead people! They knew the people were dead. The computers even said they were dead. But they kept on mailing those checks! The auditors looking into the situation also discovered 165 people that the agency said were dead, but who were actually still living. (There were two other people listed as dead, but the auditors were not able to confirm whether those poor fellows were actually dead or alive!)

Still afraid to move? Can't decide just what to do so you won't do anything?

Way back in the 1950's, a man named Ray, who lived in Chicago, had negotiated a deal to buy out a family business. It was just a fledgling operation, but in it Ray

11

saw tremendous potential. He had already proven some of his ideas and he knew he would be successful. But first he had to own the rights to the business. The family, represented by two brothers, agreed to sell for $25,000. Ray had already invested all of his own money in a partnership with the two men so he had nothing left. But this was the opportunity he had been waiting for, so he set out to find the money.

Every banker he talked to turned thumbs down. He sought out several investors that he knew - but none were interested. Desperate for cash, he offered to sell them half the stock in his new company for just $25,000. They all turned him down.

Thirty years later, that 50% ownership in McDonalds would have been worth billions of dollars! Don't you know that some of those fellows kicked themselves until the day they died?

Still afraid you are going to make the wrong move? You might. But I doubt that it will cost you anywhere near the billions these fellows lost. But one thing is certain. Staying where you are sure won't get you anywhere.

Fear is useful. It reminds us to review our plans and examine all our options. But when we've finished, we can't stay cowered in the corner.

Life is a bicycle. You are the rider. You can ride hands-free and let the road take you where it wants you to go, or you can grab the handle bars and take charge. There will always be potholes in the road and unexpected detours you are forced to take, but taking control of the direction of your life is much better than leaving things to chance.

You will make some mistakes. That's okay. Just keep peddling!

NASA still sends rockets up in space.

12

Congress still gives them billions of dollars to spend each year.

The Internal Revenue Service still collects taxes.

Investors still lose as often as they win, but they are always looking for the next great opportunity.

None of them let fear keep them from forging ahead. Fear of the past, fear of the future, fear of failure, fear of defeat, fear of embarrassment, fear of the unknown. They shrug them all off and push forward.

So what if you make a mistake? You will be in good company.

So decide what it is that you really want to accomplish and get started. Today!

◻

Sources:
1. Mars Polar Orbiter: *San Francisco Chronicle*, October 1, 1999.
2. NASA Accounting problems: US House of Representatives, Science Committee Press Release, July 6, 2000.
3. IRS lost tax receipts: *USA Today*, December 10, 2001

4 Hard Work Kills!

Hard work kills. Kills fear, that is.

Sound elementary? A little too simple?

Your mind may produce thousands of great ideas every day, but until you apply effort to your dreams, they will gather dust instead of gold. However, once you start working on those ideas, it is amazing how things fall into place.

In his book **Power To Burn**, Michael Ovis tells how he and five fellow Hollywood agents dreamed of the day they would own their own company and be free to pursue their ambitions. When those discussions became serious, one man spoke up and warned the group that it was dangerous to talk that way. Once they had these thoughts and put them into words, he explained, everything they were talking about was going to come true. "That's how things work," he told them.

That fellow was on to something. When you talk about your ideas and visualize how they will work, plans will be formulated in your mind that, when set in motion, will make your dream a reality!

The secret to making it happen is DO SOMETHING!

Don't wait for a better opportunity, a break in the weather, or until all your friends agree with you. Do something now!

You want to be a doctor? Volunteer at a local hospital to see if you can function in that environment. Take an advanced science course at a nearby college to see if you can handle the rigorous academic demands. Search your library and the Internet for opportunities available at medical schools. But don't just sit and wish!

Do something toward your goal every day. Diligent effort will eventually produce accomplishment. Accomplishment builds self-esteem. Self-esteem creates confidence. Confidence kills fear.

In reality, then, work destroys fear!

You know that you would be successful operating your own business, but you lack the cash to get it started? Read the biographies of successful entrepreneurs. Very few of them began under ideal circumstances. They improvised and persevered. Their passion carved out a path to success. Remember the famous Hewlett Packard story? That company began in a small garage. The huge Marriott Corporation began with a single A&W Root Beer franchise. (Just after they opened their first hotel, they were asked to purchase a new forty-eight-room hotel in California. Mr. Marriott's response was, "Heavens, no! We probably won't be able to make this one work.") McDonald's Fish Filet sandwich was developed by a restaurant manager who lived in a community where people would not eat beef on certain days. They would not buy his hamburgers, so he found something that they would purchase. One thing these folks all had in common: they did something!

There were more reasons for these businesses to fail than there were reasons for them to succeed. They were successful because their founders focused on how to maximize what they had, rather than just sitting still because of all the things they lacked. They did something!

"Diligence," said Ben Franklin, "is the mother of good luck."

You don't know what you can do until you try. But you must try!

Don't wait until everything is perfect. It will never be! Get moving toward your dream. You may not be able to accomplish it all at once, but DO SOMETHING!

Because - as simple as it may sound - work really does kill fear!

❑

5 Extra Steps Required!

What would you do if money was not a problem? If you suddenly inherited ten million dollars, would you still work at the same place? What would you be if you weren't snared in this never ending rat race? How many times have you yearned to do something else, but getting from here to there seemed impossible?

While you might not be able to leap from here to there in one neat jump, your dreams are not out of reach. You just might have to add one or two stepping-stones. Getting from where you are to where you want to be may require a step in-between.

One of those stepping-stones is learning a marketable skill. It may not be your ultimate desire, but it will neutralize the fear that you cannot pay your bills.

As a young man, Walt Disney made several attempts to establish his own business. More than once, when his plans failed, he returned to his old job. Drawing and writing for someone else was not his aim in life, but he used those

17

skills to pay the bills while he revised his plan for success. When a new opportunity came along, he jumped at it. Eventually, his persistence and efforts paid off.

John Grisham was a lawyer who wanted to be a writer - whose story is fast becoming a legend. He wrote each morning from five until nine. He then practiced law the rest of the day, sometimes working late into the night. When he finally finished his first book, no publisher would buy it. So John Grisham had it printed and traveled from town to town selling it out of the trunk of his car.

Some entertainers, like Vince Gill, played in someone else's band for years before they got their big break. Others worked as waitresses and cab drivers - anything to pay the bills while they worked on their dream.

Delivering pizza and cleaning carpet may not be glamorous jobs, but such menial tasks have frequently been the gateway to a prosperous future for dreamers who realized they could build a road to success one stone at a time.

Sometimes the path to success requires more than just getting a job. Delivering pizzas may provide all a single college student needs, but a parent with a couple of children to take care of will find it difficult to survive on those wages. But even that person can defeat fear by creating stepping stones to success.

A factory worker might learn mechanical skills. An office clerk could become an expert on business software. An administrative assistant might find an associate willing to teach computer networking and maintenance.

An observant person will see an opportunity. A determined person will leap at it!

Regardless of your economic status or long-term goals, every person should learn a marketable skill. Not only does

18

that acquisition bring you confidence that you can pay your own way in life, but it provides a feeling of accomplishment that will push you one step higher on the ladder of maturity. Most people need that sense of self-worth and confidence before they will feel that they are complete as a person.

Fear is free to roam the mind of the dependant and insecure. Having a marketable skill will lead you to independence and security. Fear cannot live with that.

❑

6 Want To Be A Millionaire?

Let me introduce you to some friends.

Toby is 38 years old, has a wife and two children. Toby is a junior partner at one of the most prestigious law firms in town, where he earns $450,000 a year. His family just moved into a new home in a gated community that has its own private golf course and exercise club. This 9,200 square feet masterpiece includes an indoor swimming pool that overlooks the 16th hole. The closet in the master suite is a full-size replica of Hilburn's Clothiers showroom, the exclusive shop he and Brenda lived near while attending law school, but could never afford to patronize. Both two-car garages are full. On Toby's side, his new Jaguar sits next to his restored 1949 Ford. On his wife's side, Brenda keeps her new Escalade parked beside the 1967 Thunderbird, in mint condition, that Toby gave her on her 35th birthday.

The family enjoys the lifestyle Toby's position affords. They always vacation at exotic hide-a-ways, their children attend the finest private schools, and the family regularly dines at the fine restaurants the city offers.

Most of what Toby earns each month goes to pay the mortgage, car payments, club membership dues, taxes, and credit card bills, but he is careful to make sure that they don't spend more than he is able to pay each month.

He used to be troubled by a recurring nightmare where he gets trapped in his garage and can't get to work for a whole month. As he helplessly watches from the garage, everything he owns is repossessed. But that dream now occurs less and less. Perhaps those nightcaps and sedatives help.

Toby met Brad the first time he played golf at his new club. Brad, who is 46 years old, is the head groundskeeper there. He supervises a staff of seven, and is charged with keeping the golf course in top shape. Last year, counting his overtime, Brad earned $61,000.

Brad and his wife, Janet, also live in a brand-new home. Their three bedrooms, two bath house sits on a corner lot in a new subdivision not far from the school their daughter attends. Having lived in a smaller house since they first married 21 years ago, they enjoy the large den and the deck in the backyard of their new home.

Brad and Janet paid off their old house a few years ago, but continued to make payments every month. Instead of making payments to the bank, they put the money into their own savings account. By the time they decided to buy a new house, they had $48,000 in that savings account. They used the $57,000 profit they earned when they sold their old house as a down payment on their new one. Brad cut a deal with the contractor to do all the painting and

21

landscaping, so the cost of the house was reduced by $19,000.

Brad drives the truck he bought five years ago. He paid it off in one year, using money he had saved, but he kept making payments. To himself, of course. He has $17,900 in savings that he will use when he needs to replace it.

Janet works part-time at the school their daughter attends. She drives an old Buick they bought from her father several years ago. She puts most of what she earns in savings. They pay the family's expenses out of what Brad earns, and set most of hers aside for vacation and Christmas money.

Brad began saving ten percent of everything he earned when he got his first job. He didn't make much delivering newspapers, but he carefully put one dime in the bank for every dollar he earned. That habit allowed Brad to pay cash for everything he purchased. He only borrowed money when he and Janet bought their house.

Thanks to the power of compound interest, Brad's and Janet's investments are worth nearly $300,000. Even after selling enough mutual funds to pay the remaining $53,000 for their new home, next year they will make almost as much in interest and dividends as they will earn by working their jobs. But they will keep on working because they both love what they do. And when their daughter, Lori, finishes college, they plan to take two months off and drive across Europe. Of course, they will have saved to pay for that trip, too.

Toby and Brad are both great guys who love their families and want the best for their children.

Of the two men, which one do you think worries the most about being able to pay his bills and provide for his family? The one who earns $450,000 per year, or the one who makes $61,000 per year?

The fellow who makes a million, yet owes a million, is no better off than the man who makes $20,000 and owes $20,000. Both are in trouble if they can't work tomorrow.

Do not use what you own as an indicator of your self-worth. Do not look at what you cannot afford as a sign of failure. Things can never reflect the true value of the people who possess them, or who do not possess them.

Toby is one month away from financial disaster! Brad can stop working tomorrow and his family will be just fine.

Want to keep fear away? Don't spend more than you earn. Save something out of every paycheck. Live within your means. Find somebody who knows how to create a budget and let them help you get started.

Manage your money carefully. Bust fear, not your bank account!

□

7   Take Off The Wrapper!

The fear of the unknown can intimidate even the strongest man. We are all most at ease when we are maneuvering within our own comfort zone. Unfortunately, life's greatest achievements lie far outside those boundaries. To reach our dreams, we must extend our reach beyond what is easily within our grasp. Author John Maxwell popularized the old saying that is so true. "If we always do what we've always done, we'll always get what we've always had."

Every dream comes wrapped in defeat. How many hundreds of times did Edison think he had perfected the light bulb only to see his work explode or melt before his eyes? Count again all the elections Abraham Lincoln lost before finally becoming President. McDonalds spent countless dollars and weeks freezing, slicing, and frying potatoes before they finally perfected their french fries.

These were eventually successful because what they knew was greater than what they did not know.

When yet another of Thomas Edison's light bulbs blew up, someone commented about all his failures. They were not failures, Mr. Edison pointed out. "I now know hundreds of things that will not work." Mr. Edison understood enough about electricity to be convinced that it could provide an economical and dependable light if he combined the right components. His task was to wade through all the experiments until he finally put the right pieces together. His knowledge overpowered his fear. He kept peeling away the layers of defeat until he found the right combination. He knew it was there all along. He just had to work until he found it. His near-misses were not failures. He knew each miss brought him one step closer to success. He refused to quit.

Knowledge trumps fear.

Every time.

Abraham Lincoln knew his calling was to serve others. He followed that nudge from inside. He had the education and experience that qualified him to serve as a representative of the people. Despite several defeats, he remained in the arena. Eventually the time was right. Everything was in place. Neither fear of defeat nor fear of the unknown could dominate his spirit. He knew what needed to be done.

Knowledge trumps fear.

McDonalds' researchers knew it had to be possible to fry a potato that had been frozen without it turning black. They knew the chemicals contained in a potato and how those chemicals reacted when exposed to extreme temperatures. They knew there was a way to prevent those potatoes from turning dark. Day after day they and their partners blanched and froze and fried potatoes. Eventually the right balance was found. They knew it was there all along. They just had to stay at it until they found it.

Knowledge trumps fear.

You know that you have what it takes to succeed, but all the opportunities for defeat scare you off?

Knowledge trumps fear.

You cannot overestimate the power of what you know. Rock-solid facts make a secure foundation. The reason so many never accomplish their dreams is because they build on everything except truth. They rely on what Aunt Louise said, or what that bald-headed guy on television says, or what happened when the guy next door tried it. If you are not building your life on the cold hard facts of truth, you will always be wobbly; never absolutely sure.

Knowledge trumps fear.

Study your dreams. Analyze your goals. Learn as much about them as you can.

Want to fly jet airplanes? Study aerodynamics. Understand the science of flight. Investigate the effect that supersonic flight has on the human body. Know the gear a pilot wears and what each piece is for. If all you know about flying is what you learned watching *Top Gun*, it is silly to expect to make aviation history. Learning all you can about the subject will drive the fear of the unknown from your mind, and will set you well on your way to accomplishing your mission.

Knowledge pulls the teeth from the mouth of the fear of the unknown.

Afraid of fire? Learn how fires start and how they can be prevented. Understand how each type of fire extinguisher is used. Study how alarms work and where

26

they should be placed. That knowledge will help you manage your fear.

Because knowledge trumps fear.

The value of a good education cannot be over estimated. But learning is not over when the degree is earned. The pursuit of knowledge must be a life-long obsession. Because knowledge trumps fear. Every time.

□

8   Be Prepared!

The Boy Scouts have a man-sized motto.

"Be Prepared."

There are no two words when used together that give a better lesson on overcoming fear.

Be prepared.

This little motto always works. Whether it is work or play, life or death, it is solid advice.

Preparation neutralizes fear.

Whether it is a test at school or an Internal Revenue Service audit, preparation is the key to eliminating fear.

Most people fear making a presentation in front of a crowd. Practicing a few times before a group of friends will make sure the speech flows and will settle some of the butterflies. Making sure your facts are well documented will give you confidence as you deliver your speech, allowing you to focus on the presentation itself.

The best prepared person usually wins. It does not matter whether it is a boxing match, a marathon, or a job interview. You can hope for a lucky jab to land, for your opponent to trip and fall, or for the whole prospect pool to be morons. Or you can decide to be the best prepared. Over time, that is the one who will come out on top.

Our high-tech society encourages us to believe that easier is better. Microwave ovens prepare meals in a fraction of the time conventional stoves require. The Internet can deliver an E-mail message in seconds, while the post office still requires a week to deliver a hand-written note.

But some things, if done right, require time. Being prepared is one of those things that demands a chunk of time. Pertinent facts must be memorized, important details documented. There is no substitution for accuracy, and that comes only through thorough preparation.

If you are going to cut corners, cut anything but your prep time! Short-cuts in preparation are fear's best friends.

Someone has defined success as that point in time when preparation and opportunity get together.

Be prepared!

Another may be more talented. Some may have more money. Others may have more natural skill. Yet another may be more handsome. But no one can work harder than you. You alone determine your degree of preparation. Preparation neutralizes fear.

Never be intimidated in any situation.

Be prepared!

□

29

9 Practice Like A Champion!

H. Jackson Brown has compiled a wonderful collection of motivating statements in his audio book **A Hero In Every Heart**. Bonnie Blair, a gold medal speed skater, describes her approach to practice on that tape. *"I believe in practicing like a champion. When it was a training session early in the season, I tried to create in my mind the world cup or Olympic Games. I practiced as if I were really there. If you practice like a champion, when you get to the big event, you are prepared."*

Practice like a champion.

There is an idea promoted by personal and business coaches that is expressed in different ways, but essentially says, "Imagine the person you want to be. Capture their successes in your mind. See how they dress, watch where they go, and notice what they do with their time. Then do everything you can to imitate that successful person."

In other words, practice like a champion. Envision yourself as achieving your dreams. Start living now like the person you see yourself eventually becoming.

Practice like a champion.

Do not wait until you are a success to develop successful habits. Life does not work that way. People are successful because they develop successful habits. You are the result of your habits. Habits are not the result of your lifestyle. A successful person does not suddenly become a hard-working person, but the hard-working person will usually become a successful person.

Practice like a champion.

Fear will not hang around hard work.

Practice like a champion.

If a drug or alcohol addict is not your idea of a champion, then why spend your weekends getting drunk with your friends?

Practice like a champion.

If your vision of a champion is someone who is intelligent and knowledgeable, why party your way through college and cheat on exams?

Practice like a champion.

If the person you view as a champion dresses neatly and classy, then why do you run around with ripped cut-offs and stained tee shirts?

Practice like a champion.

If a champion makes a positive contribution to his community, why not register to vote, join a civic club, and get involved in your town?

Practice like a champion.

Is your champion a hard-working and dependable person? Why should you be lazy?

Practice like a champion.

It may feel a little strange the first time you tee off at the Masters while playing your neighborhood course, but if that is your dream, grab your green jacket and play on!

Practice like a champion.

Remember what the great football coach said. "Practice does not make perfect. Perfect practice makes perfect!"

Practice like a champion!

❑

10 Play Your Own Game!

Okay, let's argue a while. Which sport best illustrates life?

You say football? You've got to outrun and outsmart your opponent if you are going to win. You will get knocked down, but you must get back up and fight on! The game has four quarters, so don't give up. Consider all your options. Exploit your enemy's weakness. No pain, no gain! Isn't that how life goes?

But what about baseball? It's a long game, played at a leisurely pace. Only a couple of times during a game does the action really get intense. That's when you've got to push those runners home! Take that walk! Lay down that sacrifice! Do what it takes to get those runs on the board. Doesn't that describe life?

Some would say basketball. You've got to stay between the lines. You can't just sit in the lane, you've got to move! You must be aggressive and own the court! It's all about control. Control the ball, control the pace, and you'll win the game. Now, isn't that a picture of life?

I suppose those are all good analogies. But consider for a moment the game of golf.

The club you use depends upon where the ball lies. You select the club that will allow you to put the ball where you want it to go.

Your stance will affect the direction the ball will travel when you hit it. You decide where to place your feet.

There are too many elements in a swing for you to concentrate on each one as you execute your drive. Keep your head down. Shoulders square. Eyes on the ball. Feet positioned properly for the club you are using. Grip just so. Allow the club to rotate, but make sure it comes back so the face strikes the ball at the precise point. You've got to practice enough with each club so that your swing and follow-through become mechanical actions, completed correctly out of habit.

No one can block your shot. No one can tell you what club to use. No one can force you to change your stance or grip. How you play the game is entirely up to you.

And what your opponents do has absolutely nothing to do with your final score. You win or lose based upon your own decisions, your own play.

Golf is a whole lot like life. How well you score is up to you.

But far too many people let others tell them how to play the game. Some smartly dressed fellow hits 175 yards with an eight iron, then laughs when you approach the same shot with your three iron. Embarrassed, you go back for a seven - knowing full well you can't use it as well as he did his eight. Don't let others get you sidetracked! Stay inside your own game! Use what you know works.

34

It's the eighteenth hole. The other three in your foursome have already played. They are standing at the edge of the green watching you. Your ball lies eight feet from the hole. If you two putt, you win the game. But the guy just before you rolled in a putt from the edge of the green. Now, all eyes are on you. You've got to roll the ball uphill a bit, but let it roll gently to the right to find the hole. You've got two shots. Normally, you would take them both for a sure win. But your friends are putting the pressure on! So what do you do? Do you win the game or do you show them you can putt with the best and try to sink this baby in one sweet shot? Do you stay within your game - or do you let them intimidate you into playing outside your game so they have the advantage?

Champions play inside their own game. They understand their strengths and weaknesses and they organize their game to maximize their potential. They know what they must do to play their best and they refuse to allow anyone to ridicule or intimidate them into playing outside their game.

It is your life. How often do you allow other people to make your decisions for you?

Jason and his family lived down the street from us. He always allowed his brothers to run his life. "Jason," they would say late at night, "We bet you can't sneak into the freezer and bring us back some ice cream without Mom catching you." Jason couldn't stand to be told that there was something he wasn't brave enough to do! So off he would go. If he wasn't caught in the act, he was always brought to justice the next morning when Mom discovered someone had been in the freezer! All the boys got ice cream, but guess who was the only one who got in trouble? Yep. It was Jason.

35

Jason would argue that he was his own man and nobody made him do anything, but the reason he stayed in trouble all the time was because his brothers knew exactly how to make him do what they wanted him to do. Jason gave up control of his life to his intimidators. He never learned to stay inside his own game.

Teamwork and cooperation are essential elements of life, just as they are in sports. Discipline, commitment, concentration, and determination are the basic ingredients of success regardless of what you pursue. But when all is said and done, remember that no one controls how you play the game - except you! Don't surrender control of your game. Play it your way. You will find your greatest success when you learn to stay inside your own game.

Confidence is the result of staying inside your game. Fear can never conquer confidence.

Stay inside your own game!

□

11   You Have To Jump!

Know why there is plenty of room at the top?

Because only those willing to take risks will ever get there.

Success will never walk up and sit in your lap. You must pursue success! You may read manuals on achieving success and listen to positive mental attitude speeches, but until you get up and start working on your dream, you will never find success.

Few people wind up possessing their dreams. Some are too lazy to work hard. Others do not believe they can ever be successful. There are many who believe in themselves and are willing to work hard, but become frightened at the risks they are required to take in order to attain that lofty goal they have desired for so long. So they stop advancing. Scared, they convince themselves that they are better off just staying where they are.

But only those willing to take risks will reach the top.

Are you old enough to remember Pete Maravich? "Pistol Pete" was one of the best players ever to step on a basketball court. But he had a hard time fitting in with all the kids at school and in his neighborhood. Because Pete had a dream. He was going to be the best basketball player ever and get a scholarship to college. He was determined to earn huge sums of money playing the game. He was never the most popular boy in school while growing up. His schoolmates laughed when he told them about his dream. Other players resented his attitude. Coaches, used to playing slow, deliberate, well-controlled basketball games, did not like his run-and-gun style.

But take a look at the record books. You will find Pete's name etched there as the all time NCAA scoring champion. He made big bucks playing in the NBA. He got there only because he was willing to take risks.

He risked his friends not understanding him. He risked coaches not liking him. He risked being ridiculed when he leaped for a dream and missed. But he worked and risked his way to his dream.

To capture your dream, you must be willing to endure the laughter of friends who don't understand. You must be willing to risk losing the sure thing for the opportunity to pursue your ambitions. You will never climb to the top if you aren't.

But you must also understand the difference between taking a risk and gambling.

Insurance companies take risks all day long. But they never gamble. And they earn millions of dollars.

38

They first gather all the facts. Then they analyze and study each detail. Once they know what they must do to succeed, they proceed. They know that their success does not depend upon the odds coming out in their favor, but in overpowering the odds. They fully understand the risks they are taking, but they are determined to work hard enough to defeat them!

Gamblers, on the other hand, count on other people losing enough to provide for their success. They make decisions based on instinct and impulse, not on fact and knowledge. They bet on a feeling that tells them the numbers are due to line up. They hope that chance will make them a winner.

A risk-taker never relies on hope and chance. He only leaps when he believes that his knowledge and work ethic can overpower chance and happenstance. He fully understands that he may be fighting an uphill battle, but the prospect of winning is great enough that he is willing to take that risk. He does not make his decision based on the roll of the dice or the alignment of celestial bodies. He moves only when he knows there is a good chance that his knowledge and skill will come out on top.

Skydivers jump out of perfectly good airplanes into vast empty skies and race headfirst toward the rock-hard ground. It sounds and looks like sheer idiocy to me. But, in most cases at least, these jumpers are not gambling. Taking a risk, sure! But most of them have trained well, and had a professional pack their parachute. Don't look for me to join them, but the statistics are in their favor. Gobs of adrenalin-crazed folks take the leap. Very few die.

Some day you will find yourself standing at the open door of an airplane carrying you toward your dream.

Seeing it just below, you adjust your gear. Heart pounding, you hold your breath and ask once more, "Should I jump?"

If you've built a solid foundation of knowledge and work, it is going to be an exhilarating trip!

But if you are just gambling, you had better hope a professional packed your parachute.

Determination and hard work build success. Gambling tries to hurry success's arrival by leaping over the hard work. That approach seldom works. Figure the odds yourself. In most cases, you have a greater chance of being struck by lightning than you do of winning a state lottery. The same is true in catching up with dreams. Work and planning will win more often than sheer luck. And who was the fellow who said, "The harder I work the luckier I get?"

So forget all the get-rich-quick schemes and the fancy advertisements that show the sexy girl leaning against the shiny sports car. They are just newfangled circus barkers trying to get you to gamble away what you've already worked hard to earn. Stay on the path that you know will lead to success.

You are well on your way. You will have to take some risks. But don't gamble away your opportunity to succeed!

□

12 Chop To The Top!

You made it to the final chapter! Congratulations!

So - to where from here?

What are your dreams? What do you wish to become?

Lay out your plan and get to work! There is only one place to start. Right where you are!

Success may seem like a long and perilous road, the end so far, far away. But success is yours if you will seek it carefully.

Have you read a good mystery? Remember what the police always do when they suspect the murderer tossed his weapon in a big vacant lot? They divide the lot into grids and patiently search each grid one at a time. When one grid has been thoroughly covered, they move to the next. Eventually they will find what they are seeking and the criminal will go to jail, because every inch of ground is being searched. Carefully. Systematically.

Is your dream lost in some huge overgrown lot? No problem! Just lay out your plan in small chunks. Take on one chunk at a time. Piece by piece, your dream will materialize. A watermelon is difficult to enjoy if you try to eat it whole. But chop it into little pieces, and it is a refreshing treat.

The Great Wall of China was built one stone at a time. Each of Picasso's masterpieces is a series of single brushstrokes, a collage of actions.

So is life. Success will come, not as a snapshot developed at the one-hour photo shop, but as a painting created one brush-stoke at a time. Sometimes the colors aren't just right and a portion has to be redone. That's life. What's important is that you keep on painting! Don't expect a work of art to be completed in a few days. It is the work of a lifetime. But it is done a little at a time.

And if fear shows up? Just remind him that you don't have to deliver the masterpiece all at once. But little by little, it will all come together. Fear can't compete with the little things you can do. He can only intimidate you with the things that seem too big for you to accomplish. Each time you divide your huge goal into small tasks, you are chopping fear into little bitty pieces.

Keep dividing! Keep chopping!

You will find success!

□

What do you think?

Was this book helpful?
Was it fun to read?

We want to hear from you!

Please visit us online or send a note to the address below.

www.sevenorders.com

Seven Orders Press
PO Box 283
Dyersburg, TN 38025

About Seven Orders Press

Navigators once plotted their courses by relying on lighthouses that were built along the coasts. Besides giving direction, the beams sent from these unique structures protected sea travelers from the dangerous rocks and currents that lurked just out of sight.

The best lighthouses were equipped with a special lens developed by Augustin Fresnel. Mr. Fresnel never patented his invention and all the world was free to use this powerful lens.

Lighthouses located on the coasts needed a large and bright lens. Those situated on bays required a smaller light. The lighthouses that served the Great Lakes needed something in between. The size of the lens was called the Order. The biggest and brightest was a First Order lens. The smallest was the Sixth Order. The one designed for the Great Lakes region became known as the Three-and-a-half Order. All together, there are seven orders of lenses, providing a light for every situation.

Seven Orders Press exists to provide a light for every traveler on this Earth. Light to give direction, light to mark dangerous currents, and a beacon of hope for people everywhere.

For more information or to order additional copies, please write or visit our web site.

Seven Orders Press
Post Office Box 283
Dyersburg, Tennessee 38025

www.sevenorders.com

Doug Ellingsworth lives in Dyersburg, Tennessee, and may be contacted at info@sevenorders.com.

44